FLOWER PORN

70

RECIPES FOR MODERN BOUQUETS, TABLESCAPES, AND DISPLAYS

FLOWER PORN

KAIVA KAIMINS
MY LADYGARDEN

CONTENTS

Hello, I'm Kai!

I was born in Melbourne, Australia, into a suburban house with a large garden filled with flowers, and this is where my love of all things floral began. My dad, a renovator, spent most of his spare time in the garden. Out front, we had lavender, rosemary, and a lemon tree, and I could smell the David Austin roses he planted as their fragrance drifted through my bedroom window.

Fresh flowers were a constant theme of my early years. Thanks to my Latvian heritage, it was customary to celebrate every occasion with them, from birthdays to anniversaries. They were everywhere: we took bouquets to greet friends at the airport, wore floral crowns for midsummer, and hung wreaths at Christmas. My mum always brought freshly cut flowers into the house and I still have strong memories of the freesias and lilies she would arrange in our kitchen.

But it was when I moved to London that I considered a career in floristry. Spontaneously, I booked myself onto a course in Covent Garden, and within the month had dived head first into this new world. The course was very traditional, and my rebellious attitude and messy, unconventional creations came under criticism as I challenged ideas about colours and styles.

After graduating, I interned everywhere I could to get experience. I worked in London (including a stint at Liberty) and then in New York, where I freelanced for some of the city's top-tier designers. I saw first-hand what full creative freedom looked like, and from there, I was able to develop my unique style.

MY LADYGARDEN

After living and working in New York, I wanted to bring the city's inventive and sculptural approach to floral design back to London. I returned determined to inject fun into the traditional world of floristry and started a floral design studio called My Ladygarden. Since starting out in my kitchen in Hackney in 2020, My Ladygarden has grown astronomically – I create for brands, events, and weddings, run workshops and a flower school, and I now have an open studio in Islington and an online store.

My Ladygarden is more than just a florist: at its core, it's a celebration of colour, creativity, and experimental design. *Flower Porn* shares my passion for this playful, modern approach to floristry. I hope it will transform your love for flowers into a crafted, hands-on skill.

The life of a florist

The life of a florist is intriguing. People often say, "It must be so calming to play with flowers all day." But it's not easy work! There are hours of heavy lifting, loading vans, unloading vans, going up tricky loading bays, quickly getting over your fear of heights to climb up crazily tall ladders, and the spreadsheets. Oh, the spreadsheets! It's not (ahem) all roses...

But, jokes aside, it truly is one of the most beautiful forms of self-expression, and with a great team, glorious flowers, and fun briefs, it's all worth it. You get a sense of instant gratification from preparing your blooms. When you're in the flow of creating, with your favourite music playing, beautiful colours all around you, and the sun shining, it is hard not to pinch yourself with gratitude.

My Ladygarden has grown at incredible speed, evolving at every turn. From my kitchen in Hackney Central to the spare room of my flat in Hackney Downs, and from the first tiny unit in Dalston to my current two-level space in Islington, no two days in (or out of!) the studio are ever the same.

On some days I find myself preparing quotes and taking calls with clients. On others, I'm suspending chicken wire at event venues to bring an installation to life. I have learned that there are certain items you should never leave the studio without: secateurs and scissors, a dustpan and brush, refuse bags, cable ties, a first aid kit, coffee, and a good attitude! One of the most important lessons for any florist to learn is to (try and) always stay calm, as inevitably, some things will not go to plan. We're quick to think on our feet and problem-solve. And that's partly what makes it so fun. There's always a new challenge. And for someone with an endless stream of ideas, it's perfect.

We live in an era where you can create floristry, floral art, floral design – whichever name you prefer – however you like. Gone are the days when Valentine's Day was strictly about red roses, and Mother's Day was confined to pink and yellow tones. Floristry truly is a personal form of expression, and it connects you to those who receive your creations like nothing else I've ever experienced.

A modern approach to
FLORAL DESIGN

Taking a step back from traditional "rules", Flower Porn immerses you in the world of floral design by celebrating the seasons and – crucially – colour. The techniques and flower recipes in this book are intended to inspire and encourage florists of all levels. Let's get started...

The designs in these pages centre around playful colour palettes and the time of year. I work with tonal-inspired aesthetics in mind and my creations alter with the seasons as different blooms become available.

While the florals and colours change, every design remains true to my joyful signature style. No matter what level of floristry experience you have, this book will give you the confidence to find *your* style and engage with your creative side.

THE FOUNDATIONS

It's time to grab some flowers and have a play! First up, the flower key (overleaf) walks you through the four key elements to consider when you're creating. It's my floral 101 and will help you put together beautiful, atmospheric arrangements.

Next, it's practical "mechanics" – the materials, tools, and techniques you'll need to support your flowers and hold them in place. The how-to guides you'll find in the Techniques chapter teach you core floristry skills and provide general tips and design advice, so you can be imaginative with your own arrangements and confidently recreate – or customize – the projects in the seasonal chapters.

I'll show you how to create five signature designs: a spiralled bouquet, a vase arrangement, a statement arrangement, a tablescape, and a suspended cloud. You'll also find bonus instructions for a timeless flower crown and a cute, contemporary buttonhole.

Spring, Summer, Autumn, and Winter bring everything together. Inspired by my time in Melbourne, London, New York, and Paris – and the delicious food and drinks I enjoyed there! – these chapters are filled with my crafted colour palettes, favourite seasonal florals, and more than 20 unique flower recipes. I hope you'll enjoy making the designs you'll find here – or that you'll use them as inspiration for your own creations. Colour is central to my work and these chapters also explore how my palettes resonate with memory and meaning. For advice on putting colour palettes together, turn to pages 162–165.

THE FLOWERS

I source my flowers from several commercial suppliers, plus my local flower market. Find my top tips on making the most of a trip to a market near you on page 166. Finally, the directory on pages 168–175 showcases substitutes you can make so you can use the florals you find at your local florist – or ones you can forage – to stay true to the aesthetic of the recipes.

Flower Porn
FLOWER KEY

The floral designs in this book have a mix of blooms with different qualities: structural, textural, statement, and small. When you work with these four elements in mind and combine them with intention, you'll instantly elevate your creation.

Each flower recipe in this book features a combination of these elements (although not every recipe includes all four). This key introduces you to the elements and explains how they work within an arrangement. The flower directory (pages 168–175) will empower you to shake up your flower selections, so you can work with what's available in your part of the world. Look beside my seasonal flower picks at the start of each chapter, and next to each bloom on the recipe pages, to find the role particular flowers play in each design.

REINVENT YOUR FLORALS

The same flower can bring different qualities to different designs. For instance, a carnation might be the perfect small bloom for a hand-tied bouquet, while in a statement arrangement, carnations might be placed in a cluster to add a textural element. Play around with flowers and their function as you create.

STRUCTURAL

Structural moments are so important. Often used to create the base of an arrangement, they are the starting point for many of my signature designs. My go-to flower is usually a hydrangea, but dahlias, delphiniums, and anthuriums work well too.

TEXTURAL

Layer these flowers to add dimension and a tactile quality to your work. You'll find varying flower sizes in this category, from bold fritillaries and firework-like gypsophila to dreamy asparagus fern and floofy smoke bush. Textural blooms are incredibly powerful and will help you create interesting and dynamic designs.

STATEMENT

The big boys – the razzamatazz of the flower world! We're talking about the larger-than-life, exciting, and wacky flowers that love to steal the show. And we love them for it. Orchids, peonies, anthuriums, calla lilies, and roses often take this starring role.

SMALL

A bloom like a gerbera, safflower, ranunculus, or lisianthus will help to fill gaps within your arrangements – their heads can fit into the smallest spaces! You should also use small blooms when working on delicate items, such as buttonholes and flower crowns, as they're easier to manipulate.

TECHNIQUES

Get the
TOOLS

Here are some handy tools that will help you on your floral journey.

Heavy-duty fishing wire will help you create the illusion of a floating floral cloud; it is invisible at a distance and can support weights up to 5kg/11lb.

Pot tape is used to create a grid over the mouth of a vase to support your stems. It's super tacky and sturdy, but it doesn't stick to itself when wet, so make sure the vase is clean and dry before you begin.

Floral tape, made of paper and self-adhesive when stretched, is used to tape stems together. It's ideal for delicate pieces like buttonholes.

Chicken wire is used to create support structures for your flowers; scrunch it together to make loops for the stems to sit in.

Stub wire comes in various thicknesses. It's used to create the base of flower crowns and traditionally for wiring buttonholes.

Floral frogs, a.k.a. Kenzan flower frogs or ikebana pin holders, are used to create dramatic lines in designs.

Cable ties strengthen the chicken wire structures that support suspended clouds (pages 54–57).

Twine is used when making hand-tied bouquets to tie the stems together. Three wraps around the bunch with a double knot should do the trick.

Secateurs are essential, so invest in a good pair. Look after them and be careful – they are sharp!

Rose strippers are handy when you're conditioning roses. When the little bumps are dragged along a stem, they remove leaves and thorns without hurting your hands.

OTHER USEFUL ITEMS

Floral gum, a.k.a. floral putty, is used to secure your floral frog to the base of a vase or bowl.

Dutch or painters' buckets are vital for storage; they are tall and will support your stems as they hydrate.

Florist gloves should be worn if you have sensitive skin, or if you would like protection from thorny stems.

How to
CONDITION
& HYDRATE

YOU'LL NEED
Sharp scissors or secateurs, gloves (optional), vase or bucket

DURATION
10 minutes per 30 flowers, plus 60 minutes hydrating

Conditioning or "processing" flowers is floristry speak for preparing your floral materials. Essentially it means ensuring each stem is clean before you work it into your design. The process minimizes the growth of bacteria that cause your blooms to wilt. Conditioning also gives flowers the chance to hydrate well, and proper hydration will encourage their longevity and increase their lifespan. Conditioning and hydrating are key primary steps for all floral designs, from bouquets and buttonholes, to arrangements and installations.

Kai's tips

As a general rule, condition at least halfway up the flower stem. I prefer to clean at least two-thirds up the stem to achieve a more flower-heavy, less-green aesthetic.

a

b

c

PERFORM

Whenever working with fresh flowers, prior to arranging.

d

1 Take a flower stem (image a). Strip wilted and lower leaves, remove any thorns, and ensure the stem is free of dirt. When working with roses, I recommend using a rose stripper (page 25) to help you (image b). Any part of the stem that makes contact with water (in a vase, for example) must be clean and foliage free. Floristry can be messy, so have a broom to hand and cover the table if you want to protect it.

The more leaves you keep on the stem, the bulkier the design will look. But as long as there is no greenery below the halfway point of your stem, you're good to go.

2 Cut each conditioned stem at a 45-degree angle (image c) – this increases the surface area at the bottom and allows the flower to drink more water.

3 Submerge your stems in fresh, clean water within 30 seconds of cutting (image d). I only use clean water to hydrate the flowers I work with. Some people use chemical additions, such as bleach, to clear bacteria. But if you use a clean bucket and water, you shouldn't need any chemicals.

4 Leave your flowers to hydrate for a minimum of 60 minutes before you start arranging so they can absorb as much water as possible. Keep them away from sunlight, warm spots, and heat sources like radiators. Ideally, they want a cool environment away from direct sunlight to make sure they last for the maximum time.

Working with
DIFFERENT FLOWERS

Every flower needs a bit of TLC and over the years you learn their little nuances, from how to make them bloom quicker, hydrate faster, or change shape completely. This comes with practice and I'm always learning new tricks to add to my little black book of blooms. Here are a few favourites:

Hydrangeas drink from both the stem and the petals. If your flower is looking sad and dehydrated, immerse the head of the bloom in water for 30 minutes or so and it should perk up.

Guelder-rose leaves should all be removed from the stems to prevent the flowers from drooping.

Asparagus fern has small spikes along its stem – take care when using it!

Orchids have delicate petals. When working with them, think about where you'd like to position them, but add them in last, to avoid damage.

Carnations were once thought of as the "cheap" bloom, but you can now find Vip varieties with speckles, splashes of colour, and varying textures. To make them look extraordinary, gently push and open up the top petals. Sometimes they open as big as a rose! (Luckily, this trick won't shorten their lifespan.)

Peonies come in several colours and bloom types. One of the most beautiful varieties is 'Coral Charm'. As the flower blooms, it slowly changes colour: from coral to soft pink to peach into a pale yellow before each petal slowly falls. It's truly wonderful to watch these peonies evolve!

How to
REFLEX ROSES

YOU'LL NEED
Sharp scissors or secateurs,
gloves (optional), vase
or bucket

DURATION
10–20 minutes
per 25 flowers

Reflexing is a technique that turns the classic furled head of a rose into a larger, bolder bloom by pulling back some of the petals to create a different, fuller shape. This technique works best with varieties that aren't too rigid, such as 'Secret Garden' and 'Quicksand', as their petals bend back well. Bear in mind that it may reduce the lifespan of your flower to 3–4 days (rather than 5–7 days). Some roses, like the 'O'Hara' variety, don't like to be reflexed but can be spun open; put a stem between your palms and rub your hands together to open up the petals and achieve a more voluminous look.

a

b

PERFORM

Whenever you're working with roses and want a fuller, blowsier look.

c

Kai's tips

If you are reflexing a lot of roses, use pot tape to grid your buckets (page 44) to support the heads so the blooms can breathe while they are hydrating.

1 Condition your roses (pages 26–27). Let your roses hydrate for at least 24 hours – this will make peeling the petals easier. I like to remove most (or all) of the leaves from the stem, but that's a personal choice. You could also remove the guard petals (the thicker outer petals) or clip them back.

You will find there is a central point where each petal "pops". Find this point and gently peel backwards until the petal "pops" out (image a).

2 Start with the outer petals, then follow their natural sequence and repeat this reflexing action, moving in towards the centre of the flower (image b).

3 You can carry on all the way to the centre of the bloom. I like to stop about two-thirds of the way in to give the flower a more natural look (image c).

You can reflex roses up to 48 hours before you work with them. If you are conditioning them ahead of time, keep them in a cool, dark place to extend their life. Once you're ready to use them, re-cut the stems at a 45-degree angle and pop them in fresh water.

A *note on roses*

Roses are one of my favourite flowers. I grew up with the variety 'Just Joey' growing outside my bedroom window, and my current favourite is 'White O'Hara'. You'll find me walking around my neighbourhood with my nose in almost any rosebush I pass (thanks, Dad, I learned that from you). They come in so many beautiful colours and shades. I implore you to find your favourite variety.

I like to remove all the leaves from my rose stems as I don't like the greenery distracting from the colours in my designs. Unless, of course, there is a prominent green tone in the palette!

Some roses need extra hydration, so once the stems have been cut, leave them to hydrate for a minimum of 2 hours. This step is particularly relevant for garden roses: the most glorious, scented, and extra thorny ones, which I tend to include in wedding designs and creations. Roses that need this additional care include David Austin cut varieties, such as 'Keira' and 'Juliet'.

How to
REFLEX TULIPS

In the same way that you can change the shape of a rose (pages 30–31), you can transform the aesthetic of a tulip to add interest to your floral design. This technique is really effective and works well with any tulip variety, but it will slightly reduce the lifespan of your flowers. Reflexed tulips should last for around 5–7 days in a vase arrangement if you keep them in a cool place, refresh the water daily, and re-cut the stems every few days.

YOU'LL NEED
Sharp scissors or secateurs, gloves (optional), vase or bucket

DURATION
10–20 minutes per 25 flowers

a

b

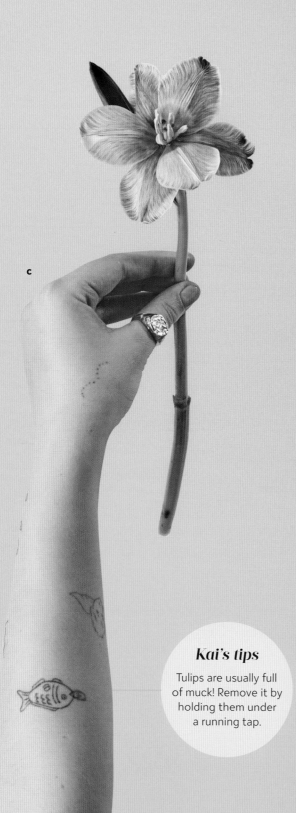

1 Condition your tulips (pages 26–27). Let your tulips hydrate for at least 2 hours (and up to 24 hours if possible) – this will make peeling the petals easier.

2 Starting with the outer petals, place your finger on the thicker part of a petal where it is connected to the stem and gently pull it backwards until it "pops" out (image a).

3 Follow the natural sequence of the petals and repeat this reflexing action, moving in towards the centre of the flower (image b).

4 Simply peeling back the petals will create the look of a completely different flower. The result here reminds me of a clematis bloom (image c).

5 You can reflex tulips up to 48 hours before you work with them. If you are conditioning them ahead of time, keep them in a cool, dark place to extend their life. Once you're ready to use them, re-cut the stems at a 45-degree angle and pop them in fresh water.

Kai's tips

Tulips are usually full of muck! Remove it by holding them under a running tap.

A note on poppies

Poppies can be tricky to work with. They are so beautiful, with a paper-like texture that often causes clients to ask if they are real! But they have a tendency to flop if they are not looked after correctly.

They're thirsty girls who like to drink too much. If you cut the stems and pop them in water they will absorb as much as possible and over-hydrate. This excess moisture causes the petals at the top to drown and rot, and your blooms will last for 1–2 days at most.

To avoid this, and extend their life, you can use a lighter to singe the ends of your poppies – this locks the appropriate amount of moisture into the stem and allows the flower to live for 5–7 days. Hydrate the poppies for 60 minutes, then cut each stem at a 45-degree angle (image a). Burn the end (the last 2.5cm/1in) for a few seconds (image b) until it turns black (image c).

Poppies are one of the only flowers I strongly advise you not to refresh by re-cutting daily.

PERFORM

Use the spiralling technique to make bouquets for gifting, or to create the best shape for a vase.

SPIRALLED BOUQUET

For a hand-tied bouquet or to display flowers in a vase, in order for your stems to sit upright and not crush each other, we use a technique called spiralling. This core skill is quite traditional, but you can still play around with your designs. I spiral my bouquets so that they sit in the vase correctly, but then love to experiment with their height and shape. Mine often end up quite fluffy and dramatic. Practice makes perfect, so choose one of the floral recipes from the seasonal chapters, or select a mix of flowers that combines your favourite colours and textures.

NAIL THE TECHNIQUE

Ensure all your flowers are conditioned and have been left to hydrate for at least 60 minutes before you start work (pages 26–27). This will make it so much easier to make your bouquet, as you won't have to condition stems as you work and can focus on adding flowers to the arrangement.

Lay all your conditioned flowers in front of you – this is the easiest way to see and select each bloom once you start creating.

The point where the stems of your flowers will meet is called the **binding point**. This is central to your bouquet. There should be no greenery below this point, as this is where the bouquet will be held or where it will sit within the vase.

Always secure your bouquet with twine at the binding point – this will help the design to hold its shape whether you're placing your bouquet in a vase or presenting it as a gift.

How to create a
SPIRALLED
BOUQUET

YOU'LL NEED
Twine or string, sharp scissors or secateurs, vase or bucket

DURATION
15–30 minutes

I'm right-handed, but I create holding the bouquet in my left hand – this allows my dominant hand to guide and shape the bouquet easily. Feel it out! See which way feels natural to you.

a   b   c

d   e

1 Place a structural moment, like an anthurium, in the hand that will hold your bouquet (image a).

2 Add the next stems at a 45-degree angle from your first flower – perhaps add more structural moments, such as some hydrangeas (image b).

3 Add a few textural stems at a 45-degree angle. Once you have three or four flowers in your spiral, add a statement bloom, then turn the bouquet around so you can add stems to the opposite side, alternating small and textural blooms (image c). Think of this as building one side of the bouquet, then filling in the back. I like to cluster three to five small blooms at a time. Once you've got a spiral going, twist the bouquet immediately after each new stem you add. You'll get the knack of this after a few tries. As long as you keep adding stems at the same angle, you're doing great!

4 Once you've added all your floral ingredients, secure the bouquet with twine so it holds its shape (image d). I like to wrap twine around the binding point at least three times before tying a double knot.

5 Cut the stems to the same length (image e) and place the flowers in your vase or bucket.

Kai's tips

Remember, nothing is glued in place – if you don't like how your bouquet is looking, take something out.

VASE ARRANGEMENT

This technique allows you to create taller, more interesting, asymmetrical arrangements. We'll use a clear cylindrical vase paired with a floral frog. The frog holds the stems in place with small pins, giving you more grip to play with the shape and height of your design. We'll also add a grid of pot tape over the mouth of the vase for extra security. I always use a lazy Susan when creating a vase arrangement – it enables me to turn the design as I work so I can see it from all angles.

NAIL THE TECHNIQUE

I find that working with one floral ingredient at a time gives my vase arrangement the most even look – and I never run out of a particular bloom while arranging! For example, you could start with your anthuriums – which often work as structural moments in a vase arrangement – and decide where you want them to sit within your design. It has taken a few years of practice to find what works for me. Have a play and see what works for you!

Positioning blooms at varying heights will draw your eye into the arrangement, so try adding layers of flowers to your design. Create three layers of a particular floral ingredient, such as a rose. Starting low down in the vase, add one. Then add your next rose slightly higher up, covering the stem of this rose with the head of the previous bloom. Place the third stem slightly higher again. This trick makes one type of bloom look powerful and adds instant impact.

YOU'LL NEED
Sharp scissors or secateurs,
a clear cylindrical vase
(15cm/6in height and
10cm/4in diameter is great),
floral frog, floral gum, clear
pot tape, lazy Susan
(optional)

DURATION
30 minutes

How to create a
VASE ARRANGEMENT

Utilize your floral frog to craft dramatic angular lines. You'll attach the frog to the vase with floral gum – put some on the back of the frog and press down gently to secure it. You want to keep your mechanics hidden, so bear in mind that if you use too much, the gum will spill out as you press down; use just enough to hold it in place.

1 Secure a clean, dry floral frog to the base of a clean, dry vase with floral gum. Using pot tape, create a grid over the mouth of the vase. I suggest a 3 x 3 grid, with roughly 1cm/½in between the strips of tape (image a).

2 Secure the grid in place with a layer of tape around the lip of the vase (image b).

3 Fill your vase two-thirds full with fresh, clean water (image c).

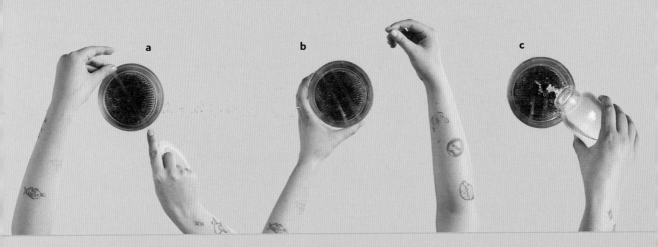

a   b   c

4 Lay your conditioned, hydrated flowers on a table in front of you (pages 26–27). To start, add your structural moments so you know where they will sit (image d). To achieve a great shape for this arrangement, cut some of the stems low, so your blooms cover the lip of the vase (image e). This makes your arrangement look more natural, and it's a wonderful way of covering all your mechanics. I like to craft the base of the arrangement using statement or structural blooms such as fritillaries or hydrangeas. Use your grid and the metal pins of your floral frog to secure your stems in place, pushing the stems between the pins.

5 Once you've covered the lip of your vase, add your tallest blooms (usually statement or structural) stem by stem. This is often an anthurium or something

unusual, like a foxtail lily. Keep turning your lazy Susan (or spin the vase in your hands) while you work to check the design from every angle after each floral addition – you'll naturally notice any gaps and know where to add your next bloom.

6 Fill in the arrangement with textural blooms. I like to use something eye-catching, like a combination of closed and reflexed roses (pages 30–31). Start by adding your blooms to the centre of the design and build the shape outwards from there.

7 Add more textural blooms and some small flowers in clusters, working with one floral ingredient at a time, until all your ingredients have been incorporated. Relax, try not to overthink it and have fun!

d

e

STATEMENT ARRANGEMENT

My favourite way of dressing a bar, or an area that needs a focal feature, is with a statement arrangement. I use a footed bowl, as it adds height to the flowers and achieves a fuller, nicer aesthetic. The combination of chicken wire – used to create a base for arranging – with a grid of tape, allows you to create more punchy shapes and land that statement look.

NAIL THE TECHNIQUE

Scrunch your chicken wire into a ball to create depth and interesting angles. A square of around 30 x 30cm/12 x 12in should snugly fit into a medium bowl or vase once it has been scrunched. Scale the size of the square up or down depending on the size of your vessel. If you use too much wire, you'll find it difficult to hide your mechanics and to thread your flowers through the loops. If you don't use enough, the structure won't support your blooms. Use trial and error to find the right amount for your vase.

Always balance the design with the same number of flowers at the front and the back of the vase. Be mindful of the weight of your arrangement – there's nothing worse than a creation that is front-heavy and falling forwards! I love to add dramatic, tall stems that are three times the height of the vase, but I avoid going any higher than that.

YOU'LL NEED
Chicken wire, sharp scissors
or secateurs, medium
footed bowl, clear pot
tape, lazy Susan (optional)

DURATION
20–30 minutes

How to create a STATEMENT ARRANGEMENT

For this look, I like to use a footed bowl as its sleek, slender base gives you room to create larger-than-life designs, but any medium-size vase with a capacity of 1 litre/1 quart will work. If you are planning to create a large arrangement and need extra support for heavy flowers, secure a floral frog to the base of your vase with some floral gum before adding your chicken wire ball (page 44).

1 Cut a square of chicken wire – you'll need roughly 30 x 30cm/12 x 12in for a medium bowl. Scrunch it into a ball (image a) – watch out for sharp ends. I like to make sure the wire has little loops and doubles back on itself so that the stems can be threaded through more than one layer and have a strong base to support them.

2 Place the wire ball in the bowl (image b). Adjust it accordingly – fill up the well so that the chicken wire stretches across the entire mouth of the bowl.

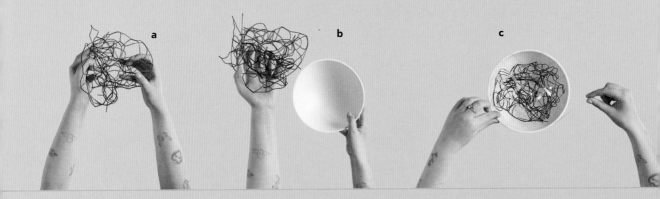

a   b   c

3 Create a grid over the mouth of the bowl with pot tape. I would suggest a 3 x 3 grid, with roughly 1 cm/½in between the strips. Secure the grid in place with a layer of tape around the lip of the bowl (image c).

4 Fill your bowl at least two-thirds full with fresh, clean water (image d). For larger arrangements, I would fill it four-fifths full.

5 Lay your conditioned, hydrated floral ingredients on a table in front of you (pages 26–27). Start with some textural blooms and create the base of your arrangement. When working with a footed bowl, I like to add the stems at this initial stage in a rough L-shape, with the two "legs" of the "L" meeting in the middle of the bowl (image e).

6 Consider if your arrangement will be front-facing or whether it will be seen from all angles...

If your arrangement will be front-facing, make sure to create a clear focal point using small blooms and structural moments. A cluster of roses or hydrangeas works well.

If your arrangement will be seen from all angles, remember to turn your design continuously. I like to use a lazy Susan to spin my footed bowl while I work.

7 Once you've created a shape with your textural blooms, go in with your small blooms to fill the gaps (image f). Add three structural moments in a cluster, such as hydrangeas. Try to hide the stem of your previous floral addition with the head of the next flower.

8 Add some final textural blooms, such as asparagus fern, and take this opportunity to layer in a statement bloom, such as an orchid, for the finishing touch.

d   e   f

TABLESCAPE

The ideal way to add extra pizzazz to your table is to style some blooms along the middle – it turns a meal into an occasion and helps celebrate togetherness. I use bottles, jars, and even old cans(!) to create modern, interesting tablescapes.

NAIL THE TECHNIQUE

Think about the season and the mood you're trying to convey: for a soft look, pick the lightest colour from your floral ingredients and match your containers to this; for something clashing and a bit more dramatic, use containers in a strong tone of an opposing colour.

Source a selection of vessels with different heights, shapes, and colours. Consider using some with a wide opening so that you can add more than one stem per vase.

Other elements to think about...

How full will the table be? Are the flowers an accent or the main feature? The answers to these questions will determine how many vessels you will need. I tend to use five as a base.

Will your design strongly feature a particular flower? If so, consider layering the blooms at varying heights.

Can you elevate your tablescape with table linen or glassware? These items add texture and depth to your design.

YOU'LL NEED
Sharp scissors or secateurs,
vessels (vases, bottles, and
jars), tablecloth (optional)

DURATION
30 minutes

How to create a
TABLESCAPE

The best thing about tablescapes is that there are so many options and opportunities to play with your flowers and colours. You'll find my floral picks and palette ideas in each seasonal chapter. Imagine your eye dancing across the table while you're working – this will help you to design with height in mind.

1 Fill up your vessels with fresh, clean water, filling each one a minimum of two-thirds full (image a).

2 Line up your vases, bottles, and jars in a row so that you can start to visualize how they will look and then stagger them across the table. On my dining table, I like to style five: two together, one on its own at the centre, and then two clustered together at varying heights.

a

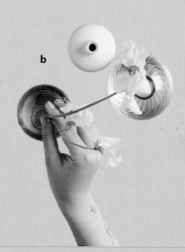

b

3 Lay your conditioned, hydrated flowers on a table in front of you (pages 26–27).

4 Time to start arranging your flowers...

Work with one floral ingredient at a time. Add your tallest blooms to your vessels first. Typically, this will be a structural moment, such as an anthurium. Then move on to your statement blooms.

Fill out the design with small and textural blooms (images b and c), arranging flowers in groups of three. Hold up each stem to your chosen container and measure the length you need to cut it to (image d).

5 Vary heights and shades of colour in one vessel, and heights and textures in another. Be playful with your ingredients! For other containers, try using one floral ingredient en masse. I like to add clusters of textural blooms to my tablescapes to create impact.

Kai's tips

When you're selecting stems for thinner, smaller vessels, it's best not to choose flowers that are too top-heavy, like statement blooms such as peonies or roses.

c

d

SUSPENDED CLOUD

A suspended cloud is an airy, beautiful display that looks weightless. Every cloud has its own unique shape. As we move from one season to the next, you can play with the distinctive, organic movement of the floral ingredients available at the time and use them as a central feature of your final design. Be creative and have fun!

NAIL THE TECHNIQUE

First, think about where to hang your suspended cloud securely. Then select the flowers that will give you the design you want. Voluminous, textural blooms, like smoke bush and gypsophila, will add depth as they contrast with statement flowers, such as anthuriums or orchids.

Suspended clouds should last for 1–2 days if your floral ingredients are hydrated properly. They need a water source that won't add too much weight to your creation. I use test tubes with lids (also known as stem or flower tubes) to

make sure my flowers don't go thirsty. We like to reuse the tubes our anthuriums arrive packaged in. Some flowers can be added without a water source. Hydrangeas, gypsophila, and asparagus fern will dry in situ over time, so you can use these stems to create an everlasting cloud!

Balance is key for any suspended cloud. Think about the shape you would like to create and take a step back from your design every few minutes to assess your progress.

YOU'LL NEED

Sharp scissors or secateurs, test tubes with lids (1 per stem requiring hydration), 30 x 30cm/12 x 12in square of chicken wire, 1 x 1m/ 40 x 40in square of chicken wire, 4 cable ties, 1 roll of heavy-duty fishing wire, ladder

DURATION
45 minutes

How to create a
SUSPENDED CLOUD

Your mechanics will impact the aesthetic of your finished floral cloud and the atmosphere it creates. If you'd like to create a more organic shape, play around with the sculptural movement and structure of your chicken wire base.

1 Squash the smaller piece of wire into a ball and use the larger piece to cover it (image a), creating a bigger ball – watch out for sharp ends. This will be the base for your cloud. Fasten cable ties around sections of the wire so the structure holds its shape (image b).

2 Your rigging point, such as a strong beam or ceiling hook, **must be able to safely hold** a weight of at least **5kg/11lb** – do check that before attaching anything. When you are ready to attach the chicken wire base, ensure that your **ladder is set up safely and correctly** on a level surface.

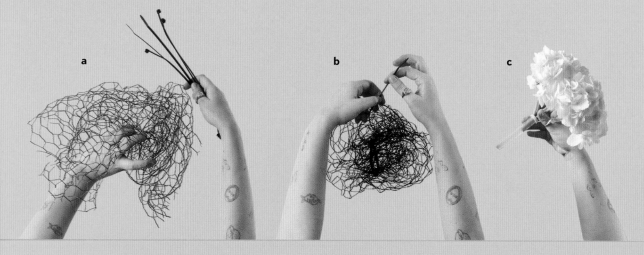

a

b

c

3 Loop your fishing wire through the chicken wire base twice – the point you choose to attach it to will impact how your cloud will hang. Tie the base to the rigging point with the fishing wire. I like to loop the fishing wire around the beam or hook at least three times and tie a secure knot. For extra security, you can add a cable tie to the knot, too.

4 Lay your conditioned, hydrated flowers on a table in front of you (pages 26–27). Next, prepare your test tubes: fill them with water and secure them with lids. You will insert the stems that need hydration (image c). Most flowers need a water source, but some can be added directly to the wire base (page 55), as can dried ingredients.

5 Add one floral ingredient at a time, cutting the stems to the desired length and placing them into the prepared test tubes (as necessary), and then into the chicken wire base. I usually start with structural moments, such as hydrangeas (image d).

6 As you build your central shape, consider the 360-degree look each time you add a bloom to ensure your arrangement is balanced (image e).

7 Clustering is very powerful. Add in each remaining ingredient in block sections, starting with textural blooms, then statement blooms, then finally, the smallest flowers. Also consider adding layers of ingredients – this will add depth and give your cloud a bold look.

8 Are you feeling dramatic? Think about adding some taller "boops". This is my floral terminology for the more fun, bold, statement blooms we can use to create lots of height and asymmetric shapes!

d

e

How to create a
BUTTONHOLE

YOU'LL NEED
Sharp scissors or secateurs,
floral tape, twine or ribbon,
decorative pins

DURATION
15 minutes

*There are so many ways to make a buttonhole!
I prefer not to wire each flower, although this is the
traditional technique I was taught at flower school.
I like the look of these non-wired buttonholes, and they're
much quicker to make. I make them on the morning of the
event, but you can keep them in the fridge overnight, or in
a test tube filled with water (page 55), to keep them fresh.*

PERFORM

These make great additions to weddings and special events. Don't forget to add pins to attach the flowers to clothes!

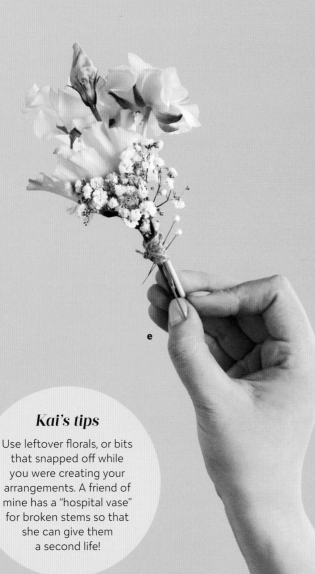

e

1 You will usually only use small and textural blooms to create your buttonhole. Lay your conditioned, hydrated floral ingredients on a table in front of you (pages 26–27). Start by cutting a shorter flower, like a lisianthus or a spray rose, to be the central bloom of your design. This will sit at the front (image a).

2 Layer your blooms at different heights, with a fuller flower, like asparagus fern or gypsophila, covering the stem of your shorter flower (image b). The buttonhole will be front-facing so blooms with smaller heads work best.

3 Once you have created a mini bunch of flowers, cut the stems short (image c).

4 Wrap floral tape around the stems to secure them (image d). Cover the tape with twine or ribbon. Finally, attach a couple of pins so your buttonhole is ready to wear (image e).

How to create a
FLOWER CROWN

YOU'LL NEED
Sharp scissors or secateurs, stub wire, floral tape, ribbon or twine

DURATION
30 minutes

Flower crowns are perfect for events in spring and summer. Use long-lasting flowers for crowns, such as gypsophila, lisianthus, and spray roses. You can spray the crown with water and keep it in the fridge overnight or for up to 24 hours until you're ready to go.

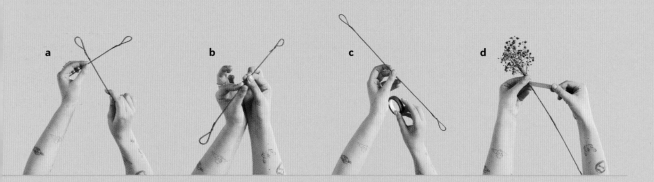

a b c d

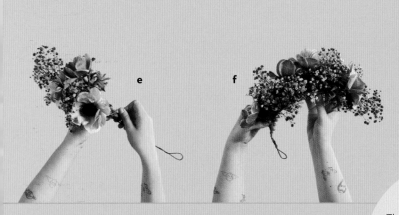

e f

g

Kai's tips

The larger the stems or blooms you attach, the larger your crown will be. Try out different heights and shapes for a more dramatic look!

1 Start by making the frame for your crown. Take two long bits of stub wire and create a loop at one end of each piece by twisting the wire back on itself (image a). Make sure the combined length of the two wires is long enough to fit around the top of the crown wearer's head.

2 Attach the two wires together with floral tape (image b). Your two loops should be on the outside of your structure to create one long piece with loops at each end. (You'll attach twine or ribbon to the loops later to make it easy to adjust the size of your flower crown.)

3 Wrap tape around the length of the wire, avoiding the loops, covering it entirely so that there aren't any bits of wire sticking out at the end or near the loops (image c). This will prevent any sharp wire edges poking out of your crown.

4 You will mainly use small and textural blooms to decorate your crown, but consider including a statement bloom if you want to add some drama. Lay your conditioned, hydrated floral ingredients in front of you (pages 26–27). Starting at one end, attach a small offcut of a bloom. Something bushy, like a textural gypsophila, works best here to cover the loop at the end. To attach it, wrap floral tape around the stem and the wire and, in doing so, bond flower and frame together (image d).

5 Repeat this process along the length of the frame, working in one direction, gently bunching together the ingredients and covering the previous stem with the head of the next bloom (image e).

6 Keep attaching and alternating single stems and clusters of blooms in the same direction (image f).

7 When you have finished, attach your ribbon or twine to the loops on each end with a bow (image g).

SPRING

REBIRTH. COMING
TO LIFE. SUNLIGHT
POURING THROUGH
THE WINDOW. EARLY
MORNING DEW.
FRESHNESS.

Achieve the
SPRING AESTHETIC

Springtime reminds me of the flower market. Dark, early mornings are gradually met with birdsong and sunlight as we head back to the studio with vans full of floral bounty. Daffodils in hues of lemon start to pop up on my neighbourhood walks around East London. The sun-drenched days with the bluest of skies fill me with energy. Spring reminds me of new life with its warm orange and peach tones, and I contrast these with lilac shades to reflect the dawn skies. This colour palette is how spring makes me feel as the sun rises.

Flower Porn
SPRING FLOWERS

Pink

Carnation 'Caramello' **STATEMENT**

Hydrangea 'Veronica' **STRUCTURAL, STATEMENT**

Allium, dyed hot pink **SMALL**

Chrysanthemum, pale pink **SMALL**

Sweet pea 'White Wedding' **TEXTURAL**

Rose 'Hermosa' **TEXTURAL**

Cherry blossom, foraged **STRUCTURAL**

Orange

Anthurium 'Cognac' **STRUCTURAL, STATEMENT**

Tulip 'Monte Orange' **SMALL, STATEMENT**

Narcissus 'Pink Charm' **SMALL**

Gerbera 'Avignon' **TEXTURAL**

Icelandic poppy, orange **TEXTURAL**

Fritillary 'Orange Beauty' **STRUCTURAL**

Peach

Phalaenopsis orchid, dyed peach **STATEMENT**

Rose 'Peach Avalanche' **TEXTURAL**

Ranunculus, peach **SMALL**

Gerbera 'Pasta Rosata' **TEXTURAL**

Lisianthus, peach **TEXTURAL**

Purple

Sweet pea, lavender **TEXTURAL**

Anemone Mistral 'Rarity' **SMALL**

Gypsophila, dyed lilac **TEXTURAL**

Asparagus fern, dyed lilac **TEXTURAL**

Fritillary 'Purple Dynamite' **TEXTURAL**

Yellow

Ranunculus Butterfly 'Artemis' **TEXTURAL**

Ranunculus Butterfly 'Helios' **TEXTURAL**

Ranunculus Elegance 'Crema' **SMALL**

Icelandic poppy, yellow **STATEMENT**

Icelandic poppy, champagne **STATEMENT**

YOU'LL NEED
Twine or string, sharp scissors or secateurs, vase or bucket

DURATION
15–30 minutes

Spiralled bouquet

LEMON AND SUGAR CRÊPES

I can almost taste the sharp yellow of the ranunculus stems and the sugary-sweet scent of the narcissi in this design. Use a vase that complements the cheerful colour palette – a warm citrus orange will tie in with your poppies and elevate the spring mood.

FLORAL INGREDIENTS

1 stem anthurium 'Cognac' **STRUCTURAL**

4 stems hydrangea 'Veronica' **STRUCTURAL**

3 stems Icelandic poppy, a mix of yellow and champagne **STATEMENT**

20 stems sweet pea 'White Wedding' **TEXTURAL**

20 stems narcissus 'Pink Charm' **SMALL**

5 stems ranunculus Butterfly 'Artemis' **TEXTURAL**

8 stems ranunculus Butterfly 'Helios' **TEXTURAL**

5 stems ranunculus Elegance 'Crema' **SMALL**

3 stems allium, dyed hot pink **SMALL**

1 stem chrysanthemum, pale pink **SMALL**

Kai's tips

For this design, I held the flowers high up on the stem, creating a high binding point. If you prefer a looser look for your bouquet, hold the flowers lower down the stem.

HOW TO DO IT

Hold your structural anthurium, then add structural hydrangeas at 45-degree angles, twisting the bouquet with each stem you add – see pages 38–41 for full instructions on how to spiral. Place the statement poppies so that they tower above your structural blooms. Add the sweet peas in a pink cluster at the back, and group the narcissi at the front. Continue adding stems following the spiralling technique. When you have almost finished, hold the bouquet in front of you and assess where it needs more height or impact, then place your final stems.

YOU'LL NEED

Sharp scissors or secateurs, a clear cylindrical vase (15cm/6in height and 10cm/4in diameter is great), floral frog, floral gum, clear pot tape, lazy Susan (optional)

DURATION

30 minutes

Vase arrangement

APRICOT BUTTER CAKE

This vase arrangement uses a whole parade of fresh spring colours! Focusing on the gradient tones, I blended the brighter oranges and apricots into the arrangement by using pinks and peaches, such as rose 'Hermosa', creating a delicious floral cake.

FLORAL INGREDIENTS

3 stems fritillary 'Orange Beauty' **STRUCTURAL**

5 stems tulip 'Monte Orange' **SMALL**

1 stem fritillary 'Purple Dynamite' **TEXTURAL**

3 stems rose 'Hermosa' **TEXTURAL**

5 stems rose 'Peach Avalanche' **TEXTURAL**

10 stems gypsophila, dyed lilac **TEXTURAL**

10 stems anemone Mistral 'Rarity' **SMALL**

5 stems Icelandic poppy, orange **TEXTURAL**

7 stems gerbera 'Pasta Rosata' **TEXTURAL**

30 stems sweet pea, lavender **TEXTURAL**

4 stems ranunculus, peach **SMALL**

HOW TO DO IT

Using a floral frog for this arrangement will allow you to use a lot of delicate textural stems. See pages 42–45 for guidance on how to arrange into a vase. Start by placing your structural fritillaries in a triangle – these stems also act as statement blooms as they are so unique in shape and texture. Add your small tulips, cutting some of the stems low to cover the lip of the vase. Using the remaining ingredients, fill in the gaps from the centre outwards, blocking the same colours together. For a front-facing design like this one, add your gerberas to the left, and a cluster of sweet peas on the right. Be sure to add the heavier stems at the back to balance the arrangement. If you're adapting this for a dinner party, make sure the design works from all angles.

Kai's tips

If you're creating for a dinner party, buy your flowers a few days before and condition them in advance (pages 26–27). The blooms will then look their best on the day.

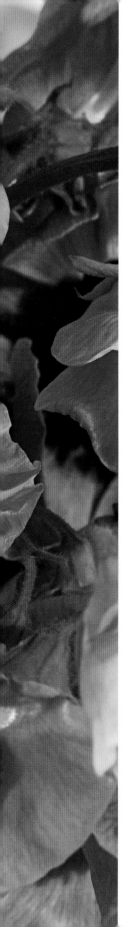

YOU'LL NEED
Floral frog, floral gum, chicken wire, sharp scissors or secateurs, medium footed bowl, clear pot tape, lazy Susan (optional)

DURATION
20–30 minutes

Statement arrangement
FENNEL AND PEACH SALAD

The fresh tones of the anthuriums and the soft colour of the lisianthus stems remind me of fuzzy peaches in a cool salad. This arrangement is perfect for a table full of edible goodies. Remember to create a focal point if your design will only be seen from the front.

FLORAL INGREDIENTS

5 stems lisianthus, peach **TEXTURAL**

10 stems anemone Mistral 'Rarity' **SMALL**

3 stems allium, dyed hot pink **SMALL**

5 stems hydrangea 'Veronica' **STATEMENT**

5 stems anthurium 'Cognac' **STATEMENT**

5 stems ranunculus Butterfly 'Helios' **TEXTURAL**

1 stem phalaenopsis orchid, dyed peach **STATEMENT**

HOW TO DO IT

Secure a floral frog to the base of your bowl (see step 1 on page 44 for instructions), then add your chicken wire and pot tape grid to the bowl. Add all of your textural lisianthus stems to create a floral base, using these in place of structural blooms. Fill in gaps with your small anemones and alliums before adding a cluster of statement hydrangeas on the right, and the statement anthuriums on the left. If you have an anthurium with a curvy stem, make a feature of it by standing it on its own, adding height and a unique shape. Place your final stems, adding the delicate orchid last. See pages 46–49 for further guidance.

Kai's tips

Don't be afraid to play with extreme scale. If you can't find blooms in a variety of sizes, cut stems of the same flower to different heights. "En masse" can be super powerful!

YOU'LL NEED
Sharp scissors or secateurs,
vessels (vases, bottles, and
jars), tablecloth (optional)

DURATION
30 minutes

Tablescape
POACHED RHUBARB

The colours of the blooms in this recipe remind me of stewed rhubarb – one of my favourite springtime desserts! This flower selection is designed to heighten any tablescape and is ideal for a dinner party. Some of the tulips here have been reflexed – see pages 34–35 and have a go yourself.

FLORAL INGREDIENTS

1 stem phalaenopsis orchid, dyed peach **STATEMENT**

5 stems tulip 'Monte Orange' **STATEMENT**

1 stem cherry blossom, foraged **STRUCTURAL**

8 stems narcissus 'Pink Charm' **SMALL**

1 stem anemone Mistral 'Rarity' **SMALL**

10 stems sweet pea, lavender **TEXTURAL**

2 stems ranunculus Butterfly 'Helios' **TEXTURAL**

HOW TO DO IT

Gather your vessels, then lay out your stems in your workspace in height order. Place your tallest vases and stems in the middle of the table: statement and structural flowers, like your tulips and cherry blossom. Think about how the eye will travel over the tablescape. Then, arrange the small and textural blooms, like narcissi and sweet peas, in bunches of three or four. See pages 50–53 for step-by-step advice. For a more sculptural look, place single flower heads along the table, like the orchids here.

Kai's tips

You can pair the bright colours of your flowers with a tablecloth base in a soft tone (or vice versa) to create a contrast.

Kai's tips

If you'd like your orchid to sit up, use the fishing wire to your advantage – the stem can be twisted around the wire for extra support!

Sharp scissors or secateurs,
30–35 test tubes with lids,
30 x 30cm/12 x 12in square
of chicken wire, 1 x 1m/
40 x 40in square of chicken
wire, 4 cable ties, 1 roll of
heavy-duty fishing wire,
ladder

DURATION
45 minutes

Suspended cloud
TEQUILA SUNRISE

The inspiration for this recipe was new growth, as buds begin to emerge after a long winter. Here, I arranged the fritillaries as if they had grown outwards from the centre of the cloud, bringing a cocktail of life and colour to the design. I utilized the shape that each stem naturally grows in, which gave this cloud an S-like curve.

FLORAL INGREDIENTS

7 stems hydrangea 'Veronica' **STATEMENT**

4 stems asparagus fern, dyed lilac **TEXTURAL**

3 stems gerbera 'Pasta Rosata' **TEXTURAL**

1 stem gerbera 'Avignon' **TEXTURAL**

5 stems fritillary 'Purple Dynamite' **TEXTURAL**

4 stems tulip 'Monte Orange' **SMALL**

6 stems carnation 'Caramello' **STATEMENT**

1 stem phalaenopsis orchid, dyed peach **STATEMENT**

HOW TO DO IT

Safely create your suspended structure with chicken wire (see pages 54–57 for instructions and design tips). Cover the left side of the wire with statement hydrangeas that have been cut short to add density and depth to the centre. The hydrangeas act as structural blooms here, too. Then, cluster together all of your textural asparagus fern on the right, and place the textural gerberas in the gaps. Add the fritillaries and tulips at the top and bottom, keeping the fritillary stems long to create the S-shape. Add your statement carnations, then add the statement orchid stem last to avoid damaging it.

SUMMER

LONG DAYS. FULL
BLOOM. RAYS OF
SUNSHINE BEAMING
DOWN. GREENERY
BURSTING FROM
THE TREES. BALMY
EVENINGS. LEMONADE.

Achieve the
SUMMER AESTHETIC

The peonies are back, finally. Dreamy hydrangeas with enormous fluffy heads are here in all their glory. The ice-cold oat lattes are flowing in the studio, and our space is brighter than ever. Mornings are warm, and days are long and hot. It's wedding season. Playful pinks fill the space and remind me of candy and desserts. Hot coral and raspberry shades – warm and fierce – clash with cooling lime and mint tones, giving a burst of energy to our palette. Summertime is fun and full of life.

Flower Porn
SUMMER FLOWERS

Lime

Allium 'Judith' **TEXTURAL**

Trailing amaranthus, lime **TEXTURAL**

Ammi 'Green Mist' **TEXTURAL, SMALL**

Anthurium 'Grand Slam' **STRUCTURAL, STATEMENT**

Hairy balls, lime **TEXTURAL, SMALL**

Cymbidium orchid 'Jungle Trail' **STATEMENT**

Fuchsia

Snapdragon 'Avignon Pink' **TEXTURAL**

Dahlia 'Karma Sangria' **TEXTURAL**

Sweet pea, fuchsia **TEXTURAL**

Statice 'Coral Wings' **TEXTURAL**

Peony 'Coral Charm' **STATEMENT**

Blush

Dahlia 'Café au Lait' **STRUCTURAL**

Delphinium, blush (short) **TEXTURAL**

Rose 'Charity' **SMALL**

Peony 'Duchesse de Nemours" **STATEMENT**

Raspberry

Celosia 'Act Rima' **TEXTURAL**

Lisianthus 'Rosita Red' **SMALL**

Gerbera 'Mariatta' **SMALL**

Hydrangea, cerise **STRUCTURAL**

Rose 'Country Girl' **TEXTURAL**

Phalaenopsis orchid, raspberry **STATEMENT**

Mint

Asparagus fern, dyed mint **TEXTURAL**

Gypsophila, dyed mint **TEXTURAL**

Hydrangea, two-tone green and white **STRUCTURAL**

Cotton Candy Pink

Yarrow 'Pink Floyd' **SMALL**

Gerbera 'Smeagol' **SMALL**

Hydrangea 'Beautensia Luxor Pink' **STRUCTURAL, TEXTURAL**

Anthurium 'Graffiti' **STATEMENT**

YOU'LL NEED
Twine or string, sharp
scissors or secateurs,
vase or bucket

DURATION
15 minutes

Spiralled bouquet
RASPBERRY RIPPLE

Is there anything better than a frozen dream on a hot day? An ice cream I loved to eat at home in Melbourne inspired the colours of this super warm and vibrant bouquet. When making this arrangement, take time to remove all the greenery to make those rich raspberry tones pop.

FLORAL INGREDIENTS

5 stems hydrangea, cerise **STRUCTURAL**

2 stems snapdragon 'Avignon Pink' **TEXTURAL**

5 stems peony 'Coral Charm' **STATEMENT**

5 stems celosia 'Act Rima' **TEXTURAL**

6 stems gerbera 'Mariatta' **SMALL**

2 stems dahlia 'Karma Sangria' **TEXTURAL**

20 stems sweet pea, fuchsia **TEXTURAL**

HOW TO DO IT

Start by holding one cerise hydrangea, and add the other hydrangeas to your hand at 45-degree angles to create the base of your bouquet – see pages 38–41 for full instructions on how to spiral. Once you have added the snapdragons, rotate the bouquet in your hand 180 degrees to add a cluster of statement peonies. Turn the bouquet again to add a cluster of celosias over the snapdragons. At the front, add gerberas at different heights to create a centrepoint, adding depth. Turn the bouquet to add the dahlias to the back (not visible in this photograph). With a final rotation, add the short-stemmed sweet peas low down at the front.

Kai's tips

A textural flower, like this snapdragon, brings depth, movement, and a modern feel when placed higher than the rest of the bunch.

YOU'LL NEED
Sharp scissors or secateurs,
a clear cylindrical vase
(15cm/6in height and
10cm/4in diameter is great),
floral frog, floral gum, clear
pot tape, lazy Susan (optional)

DURATION
25–30 minutes

Vase arrangement
WATERMELON SUGAR

The one and only Harry Styles inspired this design. Maybe even pop the song on while you're arranging. Here, I wanted to replicate the palest, juiciest shades of a watermelon, and this anthurium really does the trick. The two-tone hydrangea adds depth to the colour palette.

FLORAL INGREDIENTS

5 stems dahlia 'Café au Lait' **STRUCTURAL**

3 stems hydrangea, two-tone green and white **STRUCTURAL**

1 stem hydrangea 'Beautensia Luxor Pink' **STRUCTURAL**

10 stems yarrow 'Pink Floyd' **SMALL**

3 stems anthurium 'Grand Slam' **TEXTURAL**

5 stems rose 'Country Girl' **TEXTURAL**

3 stems rose 'Charity' **SMALL**

3 stems peony 'Duchesse de Nemours' **STATEMENT**

HOW TO DO IT

Once you have secured a floral frog to your vase and added the tape, add the structural dahlias and hydrangeas at different heights, cutting some stems low to cover the rim of the vase, and leaving others at dramatic peaks (see pages 42–45 for guidance on how to arrange). Add the yarrow to the back of the arrangement to fill in gaps and to create more of a grid-like structure for the flowers to sit in – you can't see it in the photograph, but it's working wonders! Place your anthuriums at the front, creating a textural contrast against the fluffy hydrangeas. Finish by clustering roses on the right-hand side and placing the peonies. Add one peony front and centre to make a statement.

Kai's tips

Hydrangeas can also soak up water via their petals! If they're looking thirsty, fill up your sink, gently dunk the heads underneath the water, and then leave them to hydrate for 30 minutes.

YOU'LL NEED
Chicken wire, sharp scissors
or secateurs, medium
footed bowl, clear pot
tape, lazy Susan (optional)

DURATION
20 minutes

Statement arrangement
PICKLED GINGER

These brilliantly speckled anthuriums mixed with pink sweet peas and delicate orchids remind me of Japanese kimono designs, woven carefully with each colourful thread. The peach and orange tones bring a fiery heat to this delectable arrangement.

FLORAL INGREDIENTS

10 stems delphinium, blush (short) **TEXTURAL**

40 stems sweet pea, fuchsia **TEXTURAL**

20 stems yarrow 'Pink Floyd' **SMALL**

10 stems peony 'Coral Charm' **STATEMENT**

1 stem dahlia 'Café au Lait' **STRUCTURAL**

5 stems anthurium 'Graffiti' **STATEMENT**

3 stems phalaenopsis orchid, raspberry **STATEMENT**

HOW TO DO IT

Start by adding your textural delphinium and sweet pea stems to the bowl in an L-shape. See pages 46–49 for guidance on how to create a statement arrangement. Next, add a group of small yarrow blooms to cover your mechanics. Build upon that structure to create a powerful block of pink. Then arrange your statement peonies in groups of three. Cut the dahlia stem short and place it at the front to cover the lip of the bowl. Fill in the negative space at the bottom left-hand corner with statement blooms – add the anthuriums first, followed by the delicate orchids to avoid bruising the petals.

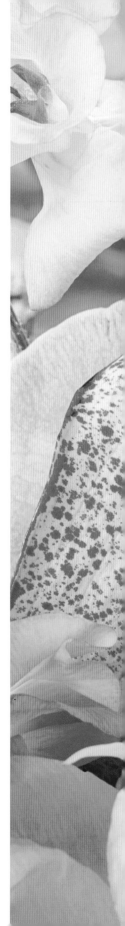

YOU'LL NEED
Sharp scissors or
secateurs, vessels
(vases, bottles, and jars),
tablecloth (optional)

DURATION
20–30 minutes

Tablescape
LIME CRUSH

*This is a tonal dream! Think lime and lemon,
crushed ice and lemonade – this tablescape is
just dying to join a fun summer soirée. Pair it
with fruit jelly and margaritas, and show off
those funky little alliums.*

FLORAL INGREDIENTS

1 stem cymbidium orchid 'Jungle Trail'   **STATEMENT**

1 stem peony 'Coral Charm'   **STATEMENT**

2 stems anthurium 'Grand Slam'   **STRUCTURAL**

1 stem hydrangea, two-tone green
and white   **STRUCTURAL**

3 stems allium 'Judith'   **TEXTURAL**

2 stems ammi 'Green Mist'   **TEXTURAL**

3 stems gypsophila, dyed mint   **TEXTURAL**

4 stems hairy balls, lime   **SMALL**

HOW TO DO IT

Gather an assortment of glass bottles, tins, and
cans in pastel colours that match your florals for
this monochrome look. Place your tallest
statement and structural stems on the table first
(here, the tallest stem is the bushy cymbidium).
Then place the textural and small blooms along
the table in height order, creating a sloping path
for the eye to follow. You could exaggerate the
height differences further by cutting the stem of
your hydrangea extra short, creating a blowsy ball
shape. For more design tips, see pages 50–53.

Kai's tips

If stems break while
you're creating a bigger
arrangement, don't ditch
them, use them to
create contrast in a
tablescape.

Kai's tips

Add flowers to your
cloud in any direction,
even upside down, to
create unusual shapes
and angles, like the
alliums here.

YOU'LL NEED
Sharp scissors or secateurs,
50–60 test tubes with lids,
30 x 30cm/12 x 12in square
of chicken wire, 1 x 1m/
40 x 40in square of chicken
wire, 4 cable ties, 1 roll of
heavy-duty fishing wire,
ladder

DURATION
30–45 minutes

Suspended cloud
KEY LIME PUDDING

This cloud is based around the creamy two-tone hydrangea – the hero flower here! Amaranthus is great for filling holes and creating shape, lending a waterfall effect as it trails. If you want it to dry naturally in your design over time, avoid hydrating it beforehand.

FLORAL INGREDIENTS

5 stems hydrangea, two-tone green and white **STRUCTURAL**

1 stem cymbidium orchid 'Jungle Trail' **STATEMENT**

2 stems anthurium 'Grand Slam' **STATEMENT**

20 stems asparagus fern, dyed mint **TEXTURAL**

3 stems allium 'Judith' **TEXTURAL**

10 stems trailing amaranthus, lime **TEXTURAL**

2 stems hairy balls, lime **TEXTURAL**

5 stems dahlia 'Karma Sangria' **TEXTURAL**

10 stems ammi 'Green Mist' **SMALL**

HOW TO DO IT

Once you have safely constructed your cloud's wire frame (see pages 54–57 for instructions and design tips), create a cloud shape with your hydrangeas, layering them at different angles to craft a dense, round ball. Add your statement cymbidium and anthuriums at the front – if they are stealing the show, snip them to control their shapes. Cluster the asparagus fern to the right, creating a textural moment, then trail the textural alliums and amaranthus from the bottom to exaggerate the downward flowing shape. Add the hairy balls to the right, creating a textural contrast with the asparagus fern. Add the dahlias to the left. Finish by placing the ammi stems front and centre.

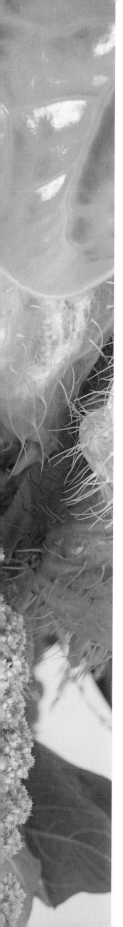

Flower crown

STRAWBERRY JELLY

YOU'LL NEED
Sharp scissors or secateurs, stub wire, floral tape, ribbon or twine

DURATION
30 minutes

Name one person who doesn't feel fabulous wearing a flower crown. Can't do it? Didn't think so – they are the ideal accessory for a special birthday, hen-do, or wedding. Frida Kahlo's iconic crowns inspired this glorious, fruity headpiece. The wire frame is adjustable, so you can craft it to create the perfect fit.

FLORAL INGREDIENTS

2 stems gypsophila, dyed mint **TEXTURAL**

4 stems statice 'Coral Wings' **TEXTURAL**

4 stems lisianthus 'Rosita Red' **SMALL**

4 stems hydrangea 'Beautensia Luxor Pink' **TEXTURAL**

2 stems gerbera 'Smeagol' **SMALL**

1 stem gerbera 'Mariatta' **SMALL**

1 stem yarrow 'Pink Floyd' **SMALL**

1 stem phalaenopsis orchid, raspberry **STATEMENT**

HOW TO DO IT

Begin by covering the end of your crown frame with your textural gypsophila, then work your way along the floral ingredients in the order you think works best. Here, we alternated the blooms for a mixed look. We added gerberas at the start and end – so that they appeared on each side of the crown – and placed the statement orchid on one side. For a different look, block flower types together. Make sure you add your flowers in the same direction along the wire, and keep checking your crown by holding it to your head in front of a mirror. Turn to pages 60–61 for full instructions on how to create your crown.

Kai's tips

Use scraps that broke
or fell off in your previous
floral adventures. You can
also use dried flowers,
which will last much
longer than fresh
ones.

AUTUMN

FRESH MORNING
WALKS. HOT CHAI
LATTES WARMING
COLD HANDS.
FALLING LEAVES.
HARVEST SEASON.

Achieve the
AUTUMN AESTHETIC

It's getting colder. Morning market runs go hand in hand with warm cups of tea from our wholesalers and treats of bacon sandwiches among the flowers. The journey back to the studio is getting darker, and the colours of the blooms are growing richer. Nature selects our palette: cobalt blue clashes with orange and amber; pinks and purples swirl into the clouds at sunset. Imagine bundles of fallen leaves piling up in the park, a heavy knitted scarf wrapped around you, and the setting sun glowing on your cheeks.

Flower Porn
AUTUMN
FLOWERS

Cobalt blue

Cornflower, blue **TEXTURAL, SMALL**

Delphinium, dark blue (tall) **STRUCTURAL**

Delphinium, light blue (short) **STRUCTURAL**

Hydrangea 'Rio' **STRUCTURAL**

Rose, dyed bright blue **STATEMENT**

Fuchsia

Dahlia 'Veerle' **SMALL**

Spray rose 'Bellalinda Cerise' **TEXTURAL**

Calla lily 'Captain Samba' **STATEMENT**

Lilac

Clematis, lilac **SMALL**

Hydrangea, lilac **STRUCTURAL**

Orange

Anthurium 'Marea' **STRUCTURAL**

Snapdragon, orange **STRUCTURAL**

Marigold, orange **TEXTURAL**

Safflower, orange **TEXTURAL, SMALL**

Celosia, bright orange **TEXTURAL**

Gerbera 'Caramba' **SMALL**

Gypsophila, dyed orange **TEXTURAL**

Lily 'Apricot Fudge' **STRUCTURAL**

Rose 'South Park' **STATEMENT**

Pink

Phalaenopsis orchid 'Shanghai' **STATEMENT**

Cosmos, light pink **TEXTURAL**

Smoke bush, dark pink **TEXTURAL**

White

Calla lily, white **STATEMENT**

YOU'LL NEED
Twine or string, sharp scissors or secateurs, vase or bucket

DURATION
15 minutes

Spiralled bouquet
MARMALADE

The shades of orange on these celosia and lily stems remind me of sticky marmalade. Feel the warmth of the tones and let them brighten up your home. This bouquet conjures up a cosy atmosphere and makes the perfect gift as the days get cooler. The petals of these lilies open over time, so keep an eye on them over the course of a week.

FLORAL INGREDIENTS

3 stems anthurium 'Marea' **STRUCTURAL**

2 stems snapdragon, orange **STRUCTURAL**

3 stems lily 'Apricot Fudge' **STRUCTURAL**

5 stems gypsophila, dyed orange **TEXTURAL**

1 stem rose 'South Park' **STATEMENT**

7 stems celosia, bright orange **TEXTURAL**

3 stems gerbera 'Caramba' **SMALL**

3 stems marigold, orange **TEXTURAL**

HOW TO DO IT

Start by holding one anthurium, then cluster the three stems together at different heights, with each head covering the stem of the previous flower. Add the structural snapdragon and lily stems, each at a 45-degree angle – see pages 38–41 for full instructions on how to spiral. Rotate the bouquet, and fill the gaps with textural gypsophila. Rotate again to add the statement rose and textural celosia stems. Finally, add the small gerbera and textural marigold stems. Cluster multiple stems of the same flower together.

Kai's tips

'Apricot Fudge' is almost a spray lily. Its clusters of flowers are perfect for adding structure and interest to any bouquet or arrangement.

YOU'LL NEED
Sharp scissors or secateurs, a clear cylindrical vase (15cm/6in height and 10cm/4in diameter is great), floral frog, floral gum, clear pot tape, lazy Susan (optional)

DURATION
30 minutes

Vase arrangement

BLUEBERRY AND RASPBERRY PIE

The tones of blue and pink in this arrangement clash... in a positive way! I have fond memories of topping breakfast pancakes with blueberries and picking raspberries for dessert as a child. Here I've imagined the two berries coming to life in floral form – delicious.

FLORAL INGREDIENTS

7 stems hydrangea 'Rio' **STRUCTURAL**

7 stems rose, dyed bright blue **STATEMENT**

5 stems spray rose 'Bellalinda Cerise' **TEXTURAL**

7 stems calla lily 'Captain Samba' **STATEMENT**

HOW TO DO IT

Start by placing six structural hydrangeas in the vase, covering the lip, to form a base for your other stems. Add your statement roses in a line from front to back – staggered at different heights to give depth. Then cluster together the textural spray roses on one side, cutting some to different lengths so that they frame one of the hydrangeas. Next, add the statement pink calla lilies between the hydrangeas, creating another line flowing from front to back. To finish, add the final hydrangea so it towers over the other blooms. See pages 42–45 for instructions on how to arrange. There aren't any small blooms in this arrangement – these flowers make a loud statement!

YOU'LL NEED
Chicken wire, sharp
scissors or secateurs,
medium footed bowl,
clear pot tape, lazy
Susan (optional)

DURATION
20 minutes

Statement arrangement

MARSHMALLOW-FLUFF SWEET POTATOES

This one is for Simon: a man who loves to cook Thanksgiving dinner. It's a surprisingly perfect pairing – just like the pink and orange shades in this arrangement. Think of the safflowers as the sweet potatoes and the smoke bush as the gooey, toasted marshmallow sprinkled with cinnamon – although it smells more like the woods after rainfall than the sweet spice in the dish.

FLORAL INGREDIENTS

7 stems smoke bush, dark pink **TEXTURAL**

3 stems hydrangea, lilac **STRUCTURAL**

4 stems anthurium 'Marea' **STRUCTURAL**

10 stems dahlia 'Veerle' **SMALL**

2 stems phalaenopsis orchid 'Shanghai' **STATEMENT**

2 stems safflower, orange **TEXTURAL**

HOW TO DO IT

Start by adding five stems of textural smoke bush at different heights, creating the backdrop for the arrangement. Add the structural hydrangeas, placing one to cover the lip of the bowl. Next, add your structural anthuriums to create a focal point – I put two stems next to each other at the front, then two more rising above the front hydrangea. Position your small dahlia stems front and centre in a colourful bunch, followed by the statement orchids. Finish by clustering the safflowers and the final stems of smoke bush on the right-hand side to add an intense moment of colour and texture. See pages 46–49 for instructions on how to create a statement arrangement.

YOU'LL NEED
Sharp scissors or secateurs, vessels (vases, bottles, and jars), tablecloth (optional)

DURATION
20–30 minutes

Tablescape
MUM'S HEARTY SOUP

This tablescape is a tribute to my mum's ability to bring us together at dinnertime. In autumn, she calls us in for steaming bowls of pumpkin soup topped with spoonfuls of sour cream and a sprinkle of nutmeg. You can elevate the simplest of dishes by sprucing up the table with vases of flowers. We used just four here, but they made the setting feel warm, rich, and inviting.

FLORAL INGREDIENTS

2 stems delphinium, light blue (short) **STRUCTURAL**

7 stems cornflower, blue **TEXTURAL**

2 stems clematis, lilac **SMALL**

5 stems cosmos, light pink **TEXTURAL**

HOW TO DO IT

Source rounded vessels to reflect the shape of the cornflower and cosmos flower heads: this will bring a sense of softness to your design. Begin by creating floral focal points with the structural delphiniums. Instead of adding a statement bloom here, place one tall cornflower stem on its own, playing with negative space. Finally, fill out the design by clustering the small and textural blooms in groups. Stagger three cosmos blooms in the same vase at different heights, interspersed with textural cornflowers. For more advice and design tips, see pages 50–53.

Kai's tips

Tapered candles will add twinkles of light among your blooms and bring warmth to the design.

CHAI LATTE AND GINGER SNAPS

Smoke bush is incredibly tactile and immediately draws your attention – it's just so floofy! I love it. It brings texture and depth to cloud designs and creates dreamy, soft shapes. The dramatic calla lilies here remind me of a frothy latte, while the safflowers add a snap of ginger.

YOU'LL NEED

Sharp scissors or secateurs, 35–40 test tubes with lids, 30 x 30cm/12 x 12in square of chicken wire, 1 x 1m/ 40 x 40in square of chicken wire, 4 cable ties, 1 roll of heavy-duty fishing wire, ladder

DURATION

35–45 minutes

FLORAL INGREDIENTS

3 stems hydrangea 'Rio' **STRUCTURAL**

20 stems smoke bush, dark pink **TEXTURAL**

5 stems safflower, orange **TEXTURAL**

6 stems delphinium, dark blue (tall) **STRUCTURAL**

2 stems calla lily, white **STATEMENT**

HOW TO DO IT

See pages 54–57 to construct the cloud's wire frame, and for more design tips. Start to build a cloud-like shape by placing hydrangea stems around the frame. Add the rest of the ingredients in block sections, starting with the textural smoke bush and safflower stems at the top. Insert the structural delphiniums along the right-hand side, with two blooms hanging downwards at the front. Add the calla lilies last, extending their natural curves to create a wacky design feature. Insert the stems at the back of the cloud, then gently bend them around the centre in opposite directions. Secure them with fishing wire. Push the wire through the top of each stem just below the flower head. Wrap the wire around the lily stem a few times, and then around the stem of another sturdy flower, to secure it in place. There are no small blooms in this arrangement, which gives this an extra bold look!

Kai's tips

Cut delphiniums can create a (flying) carpet of colour. If the stems break, lean into it – work with the flower heads and adapt the shape of your cloud.

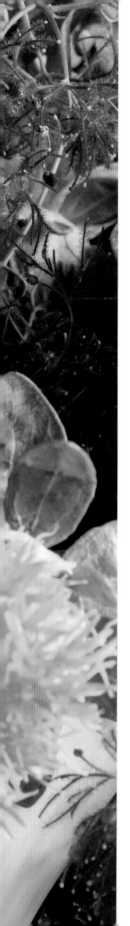

YOU'LL NEED
Sharp scissors or
secateurs, floral tape,
ribbon or twine,
decorative pins

DURATION
15 minutes

Buttonhole

BLUEBERRY MUFFIN

*Whether worn on a dark suit or a light dress, the contrasting
hues of this orange and blue buttonhole make it super
eye-catching. The cornflower sits like a blueberry surrounded
by delicious sponge. Choose a sturdy safflower stem with a
small flower head – it will be easier to work with. Make sure
to include two pins so it can be attached securely.*

FLORAL INGREDIENTS

1 stem safflower, orange **SMALL**

1 stem gypsophila, dyed orange **TEXTURAL**

1 stem smoke bush, dark pink **TEXTURAL**

1 stem cornflower, blue **SMALL**

HOW TO DO IT

Select a safflower bloom to sit at the front of the
buttonhole – this will be the focal point of the design.
Surround the safflower with other blooms. First, cover
the stem of the safflower with the gypsophila, and add
a backdrop of smoke bush behind it. Finally, place the
contrasting cornflower next to the safflower at a
slightly lower height. Turn to pages 58–59 for full
instructions on how to create your buttonhole.

Kai's tips

Pick a ribbon in a colour
that works well with your
florals. Here, marigold
yellow complements the
bold blooms in this
buttonhole.

WINTER

SOFTNESS.
REJUVENATION.
SLOWING DOWN.
SNOW FALLING.
CALM. SERENE. STILL.

Achieve the

WINTER AESTHETIC

Winter hues are reminiscent of a time of rest and self-soothing, shorter days, and slowing down. Crisp whites and cream tones remind me of snow in New York, and together they have an ice-like aesthetic. Powdery blue, moments of blush, and chocolate brown stand out in contrast. This palette of colours is a medley of the sleepy, colder months, when we wait patiently for warmer days while we sit by the fire.

Flower Porn
WINTER
FLOWERS

White

Gypsophila, white **SMALL**

Chrysanthemum 'Antonov' **SMALL**

Carnation 'Moon Golem' **SMALL**

Anthurium 'Aspire' **STRUCTURAL**

Trailing amaranthus, bleached white and dried **TEXTURAL**

Asparagus fern, dyed white **TEXTURAL**

Rose 'White O'Hara' **STATEMENT**

Parrot tulips, white **SMALL**

Hydrangea, white **STRUCTURAL**

Phalaenopsis orchid, white **TEXTURAL**

Genista, white **STATEMENT**

Vanda orchid, white **TEXTURAL**

Pink

Ranunculus Cloni 'Hanoi' **SMALL**

Rose 'Secret Garden' **STATEMENT**

Rose 'Keira' **TEXTURAL**

Phalaenopsis orchid 'Manila' **STATEMENT, TEXTURAL**

Vanda orchid, two-tone pink and white **TEXTURAL**

Blue

Delphinium, baby blue (short) **TEXTURAL**

Tulip, dyed blue **STRUCTURAL**

Phalaenopsis orchid, dyed blue **STATEMENT**

Burgundy

Anthurium 'Tropic Night' **STATEMENT**

Asparagus fern, dyed burgundy/brown **TEXTURAL**

Ranunculus Cloni 'Nerone' **SMALL**

Spiralled bouquet
COCONUT ICE

The deep reddish-brown tones and shades of coconut and cream create the perfect palette for this cool arrangement. Genista brings a sweet scent to this blustery bouquet, which is an early nod to spring, with small flowers that flutter all over the studio floor.

FLORAL INGREDIENTS

2 stems anthurium 'Aspire' **STRUCTURAL**

3 stems hydrangea, white **STRUCTURAL**

4 stems gypsophila, white **SMALL**

7 stems rose 'White O'Hara' **STATEMENT**

3 stems rose 'Secret Garden' **STATEMENT**

5 stems anthurium 'Tropic Night' **STATEMENT**

5 stems genista, white **STATEMENT**

5 stems chrysanthemum 'Antonov' **SMALL**

3 stems asparagus fern, dyed burgundy/brown **TEXTURAL**

HOW TO DO IT

Start by holding your structural anthuriums, then add each of your hydrangeas at a 45-degree angle, rotating the bouquet 180 degrees with each new bloom – see pages 38–41 for full instructions on how to spiral. Add your small gypsophila stems in a cluster to the right, then group the roses together to sit above the gypsophila. Add your other stems, then finish by adding the asparagus fern, weaving it between the other flowers. Twist the asparagus fern flower heads around other stems to manipulate where it sits.

Kai's tips

Remove all the green leaves from your chrysanthemums. This will ensure that the colour palette you've designed is as icy and neutral as possible.

YOU'LL NEED
Sharp scissors or secateurs, a clear cylindrical vase (15cm/6in height and 10cm/4in diameter is great), floral frog, floral gum, clear pot tape, lazy Susan (optional)

DURATION
30 minutes

Vase arrangement

POMEGRANATE CHEESECAKE

The fruity bursts of burgundy in this arrangement give a striking contrast to the creamy white hydrangeas. Play around with height – my anthurium here was wildly tall, so I used it to my advantage. See how far you can push the extreme height differences.

FLORAL INGREDIENTS

3 stems hydrangea, white **STRUCTURAL**

5 stems anthurium 'Tropic Night' **STATEMENT**

7 stems rose 'White O'Hara' **STATEMENT**

5 stems rose 'Secret Garden' **STATEMENT**

5 stems rose 'Keira' **TEXTURAL**

2 stems ranunculus Cloni 'Nerone' **SMALL**

5 stems ranunculus Cloni 'Hanoi' **SMALL**

3 stems parrot tulip, white **SMALL**

2 stems vanda orchid, white **TEXTURAL**

3 stems phalaenopsis orchid 'Manila' **TEXTURAL**

Kai's tips

Before you start, reflex a few 'Secret Garden' roses to give a fuller look to the design, but don't do this to all of them – allow some variety (pages 30–31).

HOW TO DO IT

Arrange your structural hydrangeas in a ball shape, with taller stems to the left and shorter stems to the right. Cut some stems low to cover the lip of the vase. Add your tall anthuriums to the centre, then add your 'White O'Hara' and 'Secret Garden' roses below the tall anthurium. Add the 'Keira' roses underneath the reflexed roses, on the right. Place the dark ranunculus over the white hydrangeas, for contrast, then place the other stems. Finally, place the vanda orchid on the left, and a pink cluster of phalaenopsis orchids at the bottom left. See pages 42–45 for guidance on how to arrange.

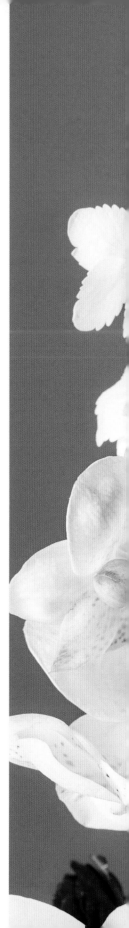

YOU'LL NEED
Chicken wire, sharp scissors
or secateurs, medium
footed bowl, clear pot
tape, lazy Susan (optional)

DURATION
20–30 minutes

Statement arrangement

CREAMY MERINGUE

I love the way orchids can bring shape and definition to an arrangement, but also a sugary softness, as their layers of petals add a delicate touch. The blue dye that has seeped into each petal here reminds me of ribbons of food colouring bonding with half-whipped cream.

FLORAL INGREDIENTS

5 stems delphinium, baby blue (short) **TEXTURAL**

5 stems gypsophila, white **SMALL**

1 stem carnation 'Moon Golem' **SMALL**

7 stems chrysanthemum 'Antonov' **SMALL**

5 stems hydrangea, white **STRUCTURAL**

5 stems anthurium 'Aspire' **STRUCTURAL**

10 stems tulips, dyed blue **STRUCTURAL**

5 stems asparagus fern, dyed white **TEXTURAL**

2 stems phalaenopsis orchid, white **TEXTURAL**

2 stems phalaenopsis, dyed blue **STATEMENT**

HOW TO DO IT

Place your textural delphiniums in a reversed L-shape, with the top of the "L" on the right-hand side, and the bottom of the "L" on the left (see pages 46–49 for full instructions). Then fill in the gaps with your small gypsophila, carnation, and chrysanthemum stems. If you have a tall carnation, keep the stem long and create an eye-catching moment, as we did here. Add each of your structural blooms in clusters of three. Create drama with some high asparagus fern stems to the left, then finish by adding your delicate orchids front and centre.

Kai's tips

Consider using blocks of different tones and colours – I like to cluster anthuriums together to give the arrangement more depth and visual impact.

YOU'LL NEED
Sharp scissors or secateurs,
vessels (vases, bottles, and
jars), tablecloth (optional)

DURATION
30 minutes

Tablescape
CITRUS MEDLEY

*One of my favourite things to do during the colder months
is to host Sunday meals. I love cooking, styling the table,
embracing comfort food, gathering friends, catching up,
and staying toasty indoors. Styling a tablescape with citrus
fruits is a great way to add texture and a pop of colour.*

FLORAL INGREDIENTS

10 stems tulips, dyed blue **STRUCTURAL**

1 stem anthurium 'Aspire' **STRUCTURAL**

3 stems phalaenopsis orchid 'Manila' **STATEMENT**

4 stems vanda orchid, two-tone
pink and white **TEXTURAL**

4 stems rose 'White O'Hara' **STATEMENT**

6 stems rose 'Secret Garden' **STATEMENT**

1 stem gypsophila, white **SMALL**

6–8 stems ranunculus Cloni 'Hanoi' **SMALL**

HOW TO DO IT

For this tablescape, source clear glass bud vases in
different heights and shapes. Reflex your roses before
you start designing. Lay out your flowers and vases
before placing your tallest stems at intervals along the
table: the structural tulips and anthurium, and both
types of orchid. Arrange the rest of the blooms in groups
of three, varying the stem heights in each vase – and
grouping some by colour. Follow the guide on pages
50–53 for more advice on how to style your tablescape.

YOU'LL NEED

Sharp scissors or secateurs, 35–40 test tubes with lids, 30 x 30cm/12 x 12in square of chicken wire, 1 x 1m/ 40 x 40in square of chicken wire, 4 cable ties, 1 roll of heavy-duty fishing wire, ladder

DURATION

45 minutes

Suspended cloud

BLACK FOREST GATEAU

Floral clouds are perfect for creating eye-catching trailing moments. The downward movement of the bleached amaranthus is balanced here by the tall, cherry-coloured anthurium and spongy asparagus fern on the opposite side, oozing layers of richness!

FLORAL INGREDIENTS

15–20 stems hydrangea, white **STRUCTURAL**

40 stems asparagus fern, dyed burgundy/brown **TEXTURAL**

5 bunches trailing amaranthus, bleached white and dried **TEXTURAL**

12 stems anthurium 'Tropic Night' **STATEMENT**

2 stems phalaenopsis orchid, white **TEXTURAL**

5 stems ranunculus **Cloni** 'Nerone' **SMALL**

HOW TO DO IT

Safely create the wire base of your cloud (see pages 54–57 for full instructions and design tips), then add one ingredient at a time, cutting each stem just before you place it into the base. Add the structural hydrangeas first, starting low and building upwards, then cluster the asparagus fern on the right. On the left, group the amaranthus stems so that they hang downwards, then cluster the anthuriums above them, leaving one standing tall to contrast with the trailing amaranthus. Finally, place the textural orchids front and centre, then dot the small ranunculus stems among the asparagus fern to fill gaps and add visual variety.

Floristry
THROUGH
THE SEASONS

As we travel through the seasons, we see colours change and develop. The pastel shades of spring turn to fiery, bold hues in the summertime before autumn welcomes in a medley of deep, rich tones, and winter brings a calm, cool palette.

Your creations will differ from one season to the next as some flowers begin to bloom and others stop. Even though availability changes, the aesthetic of your designs can remain true to your style all year round.

I enjoy playing around with the colours I can source, throwing together more dynamic – and traditionally questionable – hues. This is what my approach is all about: experimenting and thinking of new and interesting ways to play with colour.

I hope this book inspires you to indulge in and play with the beauty of the seasons too.

Creating your COLOUR PALETTE

Colour is central to how we work with flowers in this book. In fact, colour is arguably always the most important factor in creating a visually powerful design. It's key to my signature style: from the joyful vases I place on my kitchen counter to the flower recipes in the seasonal chapters, and from creative briefs for brands to floral fantasies for wedding installations, colour is king. Whether you're looking to put together an arrangement to complement your living space, match a beautiful bloom with your shade of lipstick, or find the perfect petals to pair with a dinner party menu, you have to dream up your palette before choosing your flowers.

DREAM IN COLOUR

You can order flowers by colour, but you cannot order flowers and expect them to always arrive in the same shade of that colour – even when you're ordering the same bloom! One week I'll choose a particular ranunculus with peach tones, but when I buy it the following week the tones are yellow. What can you do?

Flowers – aside from our darling dyed products – will be a shade (if not several shades) different each time, and you can never rely on them to be a specific shade. However, if you create your colour palette before you buy, you can

rely on your eye to choose the blooms that match the palette you have in mind – or even create swatches to guide you.

ESTABLISH YOUR PALETTE

So, when you're designing for an event or celebration – like Christmas, Thanksgiving, or a special birthday – and want to add an extra floral touch, the first task is to establish your palette. Sure, think about which blooms you love and don't love, but how do you achieve something glorious? You figure out the floral palette by creating a mood board based on the key colour. Find my tips on creating a mood board on page 165.

COMMUNICATE MOOD

Colour is also a wonderful way to express and interpret how you feel. Feeling playful? Perhaps you need a palette of opposing colours with a neon splash. Feeling mellow? Use burgundy and chocolate shades to create a rich, relaxed atmosphere.

SEARCH YOUR MEMORIES

Every floral designer brings something unique to a palette. I associate particular colours with particular seasons – and the experiences and memories they recall. Summer... those ice-cold margaritas we drank at the beach evoke lively lime and mint tones; those crushed raspberry ices we ate on June evenings on our rooftop in Brooklyn fill my imagination with sweet blush shades and vibrant reds. So, with all that in mind, my summer palette is bright, fun, and full of energy.

Can you relate to the colour palettes in each seasonal chapter? Or do your memories have strong associations with different colours?

This book is my love letter to the seasons – written in colour. It's how I work and approaching palettes in this way has taken years of trial and error to perfect. You may work differently and that's OK! There isn't a right or wrong way to create a colour palette. I want to encourage you to practise, play, and find your own creative groove. Thinking about mood and memory is just a little tip to guide you along the way.

CREATE A MOOD BOARD

I enjoy working in tonal colourways alongside one distinctive colour pop for contrast. Each to their own, but this is how I navigate the world of colour within any floral design. To put together a My Ladygarden-inspired palette, you'll need to create a mood board...

Start with the key colour of your scheme. Make a swatch and put this in the middle of the board. This will be your central tone.

Visualize a flower in the key colour and think about the other colours within the bloom. If you picture an anthurium, for example, perhaps it has a yellow or pink stamen; perhaps there's an ombré effect as one shade transitions into another. If you select flowers that match the tones found within the anthurium stem, they will work well within the palette.

Use a colour wheel to help you (you can find colour wheels online or even in decorating stores). Working within the same hues on the wheel as your central tone, select one stronger and deeper tone, followed by one that is softer and paler, and add the swatches to your mood board.

Finally, pick a colour from the opposing side of the colour wheel to create the clashing moment that pops! I love how this looks – plus, this approach will add depth and dimension to your design, without the palette becoming too messy or busy. Give it a try!

How to
SHOP FLOWER MARKETS

Flower markets are a smorgasbord of characters, colours, and scents. Somehow they always have an exciting and energetic buzz. For me, the small hours, an abundance of coffee, and the promise of a sunrise over the River Thames during the drive home only add to the charm of the adventure. Although markets may seem intimidating – and at first they definitely can be – you'll quickly learn to love the madness of early mornings with suppliers. London's New Covent Garden and the array of wholesale stores on 28th Street in New York certainly have my heart. Here are some tips to help you navigate the first few trips to your local market.

INTRODUCE YOURSELF

When shopping around, introduce yourself to the wholesale suppliers. These incredible humans are floral wizards who source the most wonderful and wacky blooms. I don't know where we'd be without our suppliers! Building relationships here is, in my opinion, one of the most crucial factors in creating successful floral designs. Always be kind!

ASK, DON'T TOUCH

Ask questions – suppliers are happy to help. In return for their advice and guidance, don't pick up every bunch you see. Suppliers will have carefully sorted and looked after their blooms and, call me Miss Obvious, flowers are fragile. If you grab a bunch casually with no intention of buying, you could damage precious stock and ruin stems for fellow florists.

HOW MANY ARE IN A BUNCH?

Usually, blooms are sold in bunches of 10, 25, or 50 stems. On the odd occasion, suppliers may agree to split large bunches in half – this is a no-go more often than not, but it never hurts to ask. Wholesale bunches rarely feature prices, so this takes us back to fostering a good relationship with your suppliers, because you'll need to ask the price of everything.

TAKE CASH AND REMEMBER TAX!

Take cash! It might get you a better deal. And remember: *suppliers will add tax to your order.* Even though I work with flowers, I'm not naturally a morning person – c'est la vie! There have been times when I've forgotten and panicked when the bill was higher than expected. Take it from a sleepy, caffeine-deprived florist: it's not a nice surprise. Always factor in the tax before you buy.

Flower directory STRUCTURAL MOMENTS

You could substitute any of the flowers pictured here for monstera leaf, larkspur, goldenrod, stocks, or bells of Ireland.

∨ ∧ **HYDRANGEA**
An essential bloom!
Their spherical shape is
perfect for creating
cloud-like shapes.

> **ANTHURIUM**
Another floral hero!
Use these to create
long lines and to
add depth.

^ FRENCH TULIP
My favourite flower. Truly,
want to be my valentine? I'll
take a bunch of these. Watch
how their stems curve and
shape, bend and dance, over
the course of their lifespan.

^ > DECORATIVE DAHLIA
Buy dahlias like 'Café au Lait' on the
morning you want to use them as they can
flop unexpectedly. They love to drink –
treat them like the princesses they are by
making sure their water is cool and clean.

Flower directory
TEXTURAL BLOOMS

You could substitute any of the flowers pictured here with agapanthus, Peruvian lily, kangaroo paw, false goatsbeard, crocosmia, St John's wort, thistle, or nigella.

∧ SWEET PEA
These highly scented stems have a wonderful, under-the-sea-like texture that's very playful.

> GYPSOPHILA
You could use white stems, but gyp is ideal for adding moments of colour so try a bright dyed shade. This bloom reminds me of fireworks.

∨ CACTUS OR SEMI-CACTUS DAHLIA
Layer these spidery blooms, such as 'Karma Sangria', to create interest.

> RANUNCULUS BUTTERFLY
The softest, most buttery, beautiful shape comes to life when these bloom. Best to use them 3–4 days after they have been conditioned.

< ∧ POPPY The queens of the flower realm. They love to flop. Say nice things to them and they will pop open faster. Wonder at their amazing texture, and be sure to burn their stems to make them last longer.

> CELOSIA Another wacky ingredient – it looks a lot like a brain! Use these stems to create a solid base for your arrangements.

∧ GERBERA There are (seemingly) a million varieties to choose from. Their petals range from flat to fuzzy, and they last for ages. Plus, they are budget friendly!

∨ ASPARAGUS FERN What more do you need when this stem is in town? It comes in lots of dyed colours and adds volume as well as texture.

∨ HAIRY BALLS I call these hairy balls, so sue me. Whatever you call them, they're great for adding a weird and wonderful dimension to your arrangement.

< **CYMBIDIUM ORCHID** Thick 'n' juicy. Adds real pizzazz.

< ∧ **PEONY** Use when in full bloom for best effect!

∨ **PHALAENOPSIS ORCHID** One of my favourites. Add them into arrangements last, and always handle with care.

> **CURLY ANTHURIUM** Curly anthuriums such as 'Graffiti' are usually harvested once a week. The speckles and unique stamen make this variety super special.

Flower directory
STATEMENT BLOOMS

You could substitute any of the flowers pictured here for foxglove, sword lily, dried cotton stems, lily, bird of paradise, or dried palm.

< ∨ **GARDEN ROSE** As well as smelling great, garden roses make a real statement – they have a unique shape when in full bloom.

∧ ANEMONE Sometimes these come in mixed bunches when you order one colour – so don't be surprised if you get shades ranging from hot violet and deep aubergine to a super creamy soft lilac within a single bunch of purple stems.

∧ CARNATION À la Carrie Bradshaw, these are making a comeback. Push back the petals to make sure they're as floofy as can be.

> ALLIUM (DYED) Use with care as the dye easily transfers from these stems!

< LISIANTHUS You can utilize the bud and the bloom here. Both give you unique shapes and have lots of ruffles.

< CHRYSANTHEMUM
Floofy delights! They are long-lasting and have a similar texture to decorative dahlias (like 'Café au Lait'), so they make a great substitute if you can't find those.

∨ GERBERA
You'll also find these in the textural section, but they are great for filling gaps in any arrangement. Varieties abound, but when you want to add some extra impact, remember: the fuzzier, the better.

Flower directory
SMALL
BLOOMS

You could substitute any of the flowers pictured here with spray chrysanthemum, milkweed, firecracker bush, clematis, cosmos, drumsticks, phlox, or freesia.

∨ RANUNCULUS They just get better and better as they bloom. There are so many varieties – the Cloni series is my favourite.

RESOURCES

Flower markets

LONDON
New Covent Garden Flower Market
You can visit this wholesale market from Monday to Saturday. Park upstairs and head down to the level with all the wholesale suppliers for flowers, sundries, and plants. My favourite stores for sundries are Whittingtons and Lavenders of Covent Garden. Say hey to Sam at Bloomfield and wave to Paul at GB Foliage. Grab a cup of tea and be sure to nab a bacon sandwich at the café too.

Columbia Road Flower Market
This market is only open on Sundays. It's a hop, skip, and a jump from Bethnal Green or Shoreditch High Street stations. You'll buy flowers by the bunch here, but the prices are similar to the wholesale market. Wait until the end of the day for a bargain! Bring cash.

TUSCANY
Flora Toscana
This is a great wholesale market. You can buy in person or place pre-orders online. If you fly into Florence, it's about a 15-minute drive from the airport.

MELBOURNE
There are several great wholesalers in Melbourne, so choose the market that suits your location. I highly recommend a trip to Mr Fresh Wholesale Flowers or Santospirito Flowers. My favourite place, Tesselaar Flowers, has a cute farm shop down the road that's perfect for a post-market snack.

NEW YORK CITY
The Flower District – 28th Street
Flower heaven is a place on earth, and you will find it between 8th and 9th Avenues. The blooms spill out onto the streets. It's best to buy sundries at Jamali Garden – it is a treasure trove and – yes! – they have two floors to explore! Dutch Flower Line usually has the largest selection of blooms, plus Chris and Vinnie are legends. Also, give my love to Troy at J-Rose, and to Persaud at Twenty Eight Street Wholesale Flowers.

Union Square Farmers' Market
I used to go here to get locally sourced flowers from Upstate New York (if you're in town and have time, go and check out the Hudson River). I wouldn't go to Union Square for large quantities, more if you want to support local growers and get some great snacks while you're at it!

Books

Floret Farm's Cut Flower Garden: Grow, Harvest, and Arrange Stunning Seasonal Blooms, Benzakein, Erin and Waite, Michele M., Chronicle Books, 2017.

Flower Colour Guide, Putnam, Darroch and Putnam, Michael, Phaidon Press, 2018.

The Complete Language of Flowers: A Definitive and Illustrated History, Dietz, S. Theresa, Wellfleet Press, 2020.

INDEX OF FLOWER NAMES

Throughout the book, we referred to the flowers by their genus, or common name, followed by their colour, or the colour name given by the supplier. If you want to source the flowers in the book, here is an alphabetical list of the flowers as they appear on the page, plus the scientific names used by suppliers. Turn to the pages listed to remind yourself which recipes each bloom featured in.

INDEX

Thank you!

I had my heart set on writing a book, and after googling, "How to make a book demo", I did not stop until someone turned that dream into a reality.

It takes a wonderful team to create a book. Over a glass of wine, I met with Millie, who introduced me to Steph. Thank you both for taking a chance on me.

A huge thanks to the team at DK for bringing my vision to life. To all the creative team on the shoots: Bess, Jess, Rachel, and our floral assistants Sasha and Lily. To all our suppliers, far and wide, who source all the wild floral requests I have – and always deliver with a smile. Especially to Sam, our Flower King, and the team at Bloomfield in London.

To my parents, Anita and John, whose collective love for flowers inspires me always.

A big thank you to Simon, who is quite possibly one of the most supportive people I know, and to all those who have cheered me along the way. This one's for you! X

Senior Editor Sophie Blackman
Senior Designer Louise Brigenshaw
Senior Acquisitions Editor Stephanie Milner
Production Editor David Almond
Production Controller Stephanie McConnell
DTP Designer Nand Kishor Acharya
Jacket Coordinator Jasmine Lennie
Editorial Manager Ruth O'Rourke
Design Manager Marianne Markham
Art Director Maxine Pedliham
Publishing Director Katie Cowan

Art direction and Design Bess Daly at hello
Editor Krissy Mallett
Proofreader Katie Hewett
Indexer Ruth Ellis
Flower indexer Philip Clayton
Photographer Jessica Griffiths
Jacket Designer Bess Daly at hello
Prop Stylist Rachel Vere
Floral assistants Sasha Grigorik and Lily Gisbourne

First American Edition, 2023
Published in the United States by DK Publishing
1745 Broadway, 20th Floor, New York, NY 10019

Copyright © 2023 Dorling Kindersley Limited
DK, a Division of Penguin Random House LLC
23 24 25 26 27 10 9 8 7 6 5 4 3 2 1
001–332324–Jan/2023

A catalog record for this book
is available from the Library of Congress.
ISBN: 978-0-7440-6958-7

Printed and bound in Scotland

For the curious

www.dk.com

MIX
Paper | Supporting
responsible forestry
FSC™ C018179

This book was made with Forest
Stewardship Council™ certified
paper—one small step in DK's
commitment to a sustainable future.
For more information go to
www.dk.com/our-green-pledge